029.1(E)

SCIENCE DISCOVERY

MACHINES AT WORK

Alan Ward

Watts Books

London • New York • Sydney

© 1993 Watts Books

Watts Books
96 Leonard Street
London
EC2A 4RH

Franklin Watts, Inc
387 Park Avenue South
New York, NY 10016

Franklin Watts Australia
14 Mars Road
Lane Cove
NSW 2066

UK ISBN: 0 7496 1142 1

10 9 8 7 6 5 4 3 2 1

Printed in Great Britain

A CIP catalogue record for this
book is available from the
British Library

Dewey Decimal
Classification: 621.8

Editor: Pippa Pollard
Designer: Mike Snell
Artist: Ray Turvey

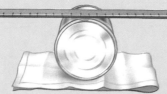

CONTENTS

LIFE WITHOUT MACHINES

Imagine a world with no machines — no bicycles, cars, aeroplanes, cranes, ditch-diggers, cookers or tools. How are machines important in your life?

Try digging a hole in the ground with your bare hands, instead of using a spade. Or imagine having to climb a pole to put up a flag, instead of using a rope and pulley wheels. A spade is a kind of lever. Pulleys and levers are examples of simple machines.

Digging with a spade-lever

Push the spade into the soil. Grasp it by its middle (between the blade and the handle). Then pull back hard on the spade. Do not strain yourself! Don't worry if you cannot dig up a spadeful of soil.

Push the spade in the ground again. This time though, pull back on the handle of the spade. Now you should find it easy to move a spadeful of soil.

YOU NEED:

- a garden spade
- some waste ground with loose soil

Ask an adult for permission.

What has happened?

By using the full length of the spade-lever, you are able to use your strength to exert a greater force on the soil.

Make a model flagpole

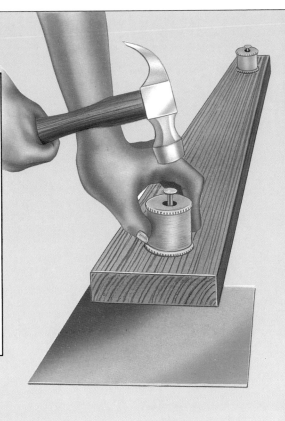

YOU NEED:

- a long strip of wood (about 1 m long)
- 2 cotton reels
- 2 nails (longer than the cotton reels)
- string
- scissors
- a paper flag
- paste
- a hammer

Rest the wood on the ground, out of doors. Gently hammer in the nails as shown in the picture to fix the cotton reels to the strip of wood. Be careful with the hammer! The cotton reels will act as pulleys.

Use the string to make a fairly tight belt running between the pulleys. Fold over an edge of the paper flag, and paste this edge over the string.

Stand up your wooden flagpole. Raise or lower the flag by pulling down either side of the belt of string. You could make a really tall flagpole for your garden.

What has happened?

The pulleys change the direction of your pull and the string transmits your force to lower or raise the flag as you want.

Did you know?

A bicycle is made by combining together several kinds of simple machine, so it is an example of a compound machine.

WHAT A MACHINE CAN DO

A machine can help you to do a job more easily, with less effort and bother than if you had to do it on your own, without a machine.

YOU NEED:

- used matches (ask an adult for them)
- a matchbox

A machine can help you in several ways:

1. By passing on or transmitting a force. Forces are pushes and pulls. You used a string belt to transmit pulls to raise and lower a flag. Here is a fun way to use a series of little levers to tip over a matchbox some distance away.

Arrange the matches in the criss-cross pattern shown in the picture. Put the matchbox end-up on the tip of the last match. When you push on the first stick-lever, your force is passed on from lever to lever, to topple the matchbox.

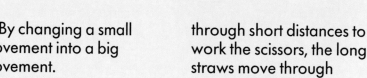

2. By changing a small movement into a big movement.

through short distances to work the scissors, the long straws move through greater distances.

YOU NEED:

- a pair of nail scissors
- 2 drinking straws

Fit the straws on the blades of the scissors. When you push and pull

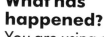

What has happened?
You are using a joined pair of levers to magnify movements.

3. By changing the direction of a force.

When you pulled back on the handle of a spade, you made its blade push forward and up to dig the soil.

Scissors consist of a pair of levers. They are jointed in the middle, so when you push or pull one way, their points go the other way.

Draw a bird without its beak on the paper. Carefully

poke the scissors out through the paper where the bird's beak should begin. Work the scissors behind the paper. Their moving points look like a beak opening and shutting.

4. By changing a small force into a large force. This is the most important use of a machine. Using the spade-lever enabled you to magnify the effect of your force. A different way to do this is to use a paper bag as a lifting machine.

Put the flattened bag near the edge of a table. Pile the books on the middle of the bag. Gather the

opening of the bag into a small tube and blow into the bag through it. You should be able to lift the books from the table. (If you find it hard to do, take some of the books away and try it again.)

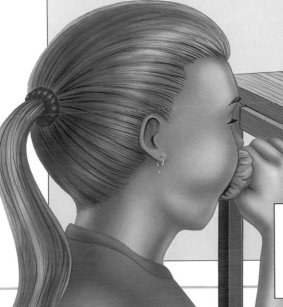

What has happened?
The air going into the bag pushed up on the books and lifted them from the table.

LEVERS

A see-saw is a lever-machine that can be tilted in opposite ways. When one end is tilted up, the other end tilts down. The place in the middle, where the see-saw is supported and turns, is called the fulcrum.

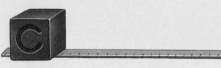

YOU NEED:

- a half-metre ruler
- cube-shaped toy wooden blocks
- a round tin
- a folded handkerchief

Use a see-saw to show how a machine can be used to get a small force to act against and support a larger force.

Put the tin with its rounded side resting on the handkerchief. Balance the ruler on the curve of the tin. The tin acts as a fulcrum. Now you can make the force of one block's weight balance the force of two blocks' weight, as shown in the picture.

Can you get one block to balance on the see-saw against a pile of three blocks?

fulcrum

Did you know?
There are many levers used in your home. They include scissors, sugar tongs, spanners, hammers (when they are used to lever out nails from wood) and pliers. Even a door is a lever in disguise. Can you see why?

Make your own 'wheelbarrow-lever'

YOU NEED:

- a tall coffee jar
- thread
- a half-metre ruler
- a pencil
- wooden blocks
- sticky tape
- a pair of scissors

Tape one end of the pencil to the lid of the coffee jar. Tie the thread around one end of the ruler and attach the other end of the piece of thread to one of the wooden blocks. Hang this wooden block over the pencil taped to the coffee jar, so that one end of the ruler is suspended in the air. You will now be able to put two wooden blocks on the other end of the ruler.

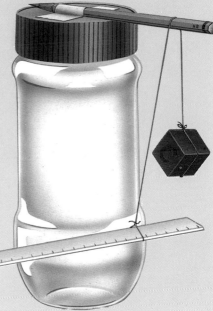

fulcrum

What has happened?
The weight of one block is now lifting two blocks' weight plus the weight of the ruler.

Compare what you have done with this wheelbarrow:
When you lift the handles, your force can lift a greater force (the weight of the loaded barrow). The wheel is also the fulcrum of the wheelbarrow lever.

A 'wheelbarrow-lever'

Levers are often rods, blades and bars like the ruler, but they may be disguised as other shapes. A wheelbarrow is a lever with a fulcrum at one end.

effort

load

PULLEYS

Like levers, pulleys can be used to boost your ordinary human strength. You used a pulley to change the direction of a force (another name for a load or an effort) to pull a flag up a flagpole. Pulley machines are also used to raise or drag heavy loads using smaller efforts.

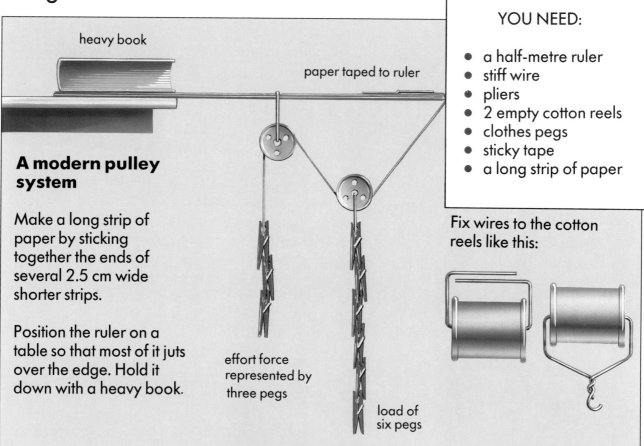

heavy book

paper taped to ruler

A modern pulley system

Make a long strip of paper by sticking together the ends of several 2.5 cm wide shorter strips.

Position the ruler on a table so that most of it juts over the edge. Hold it down with a heavy book.

effort force represented by three pegs

load of six pegs

YOU NEED:

- a half-metre ruler
- stiff wire
- pliers
- 2 empty cotton reels
- clothes pegs
- sticky tape
- a long strip of paper

Fix wires to the cotton reels like this:

What has happened?
The pulley holding up the load is being supported by two portions of the paper (representing strings or ropes of a real pulley system). Each 'string' takes the strain of half the load. One string is supported by the ruler. The other string – after passing over the second pulley – is the one actually being pulled by the effort force, which is the weight of the three pegs. If workshop pulleys were used like this, you could raise a mass of 20 kg with a pull equal to the weight of only 10 kg.

A clever stunt

Tie the rope to one of the broom handle rods and wind it between the two of them as shown in the picture. Get two of your friends to sit on the chairs facing each other with their feet off the floor. Wearing the gloves, they should each hold one of the rods horizontally in their hands. Taking the free end of the rope, pull on it so that you make your friends slide towards each other.

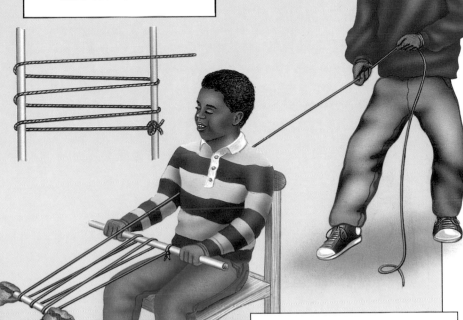

What has happened?
The rods and rope formed a rough pulley system that made easy work for you doing the pulling.

Did you know?
Pulleys are like separate hands helping to lift a heavy load, such as a table. If many people's hands and efforts are used, the heaviest table is easy to lift. As the saying goes, 'Many hands make light work.'

RAMPS AND SCREWS

Do you climb a hill by going up a short steep path, or take more time — but exert less effort — by going along a kinder slope that winds around the side of the hill?

Most people prefer to take their time and put less strain on their bodies. By doing so they are using the easier path as a machine, called a ramp.

Testing forces on a ramp

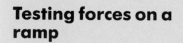

YOU NEED:

- a long rubber band
- a drawing-pin
- a heavy toy car
- a short plank of wood
- Blutac

Cut the rubber band to make a long rubber strip. Fix the pin at one end of the plank. Tie an end of the rubber strip to the pin. Tie the other end to the toy car. Stick two 'beads' of Blutac, about 3 cm apart, around the middle of the rubber strip.

Raise the end of the plank where you have fixed the pin. Notice that the force of the toy car's weight makes the rubber stretch.

Make the slope steeper. Watch what happens.

What has happened?

Making the ramp steeper meant that the rubber strip had to pull and hold more of the car's whole weight. (You saw this happen when the beads were pulled further apart.)

Did you know?

Builders and engineers use ramp machines when they need to raise heavy objects with the least effort. Ramps are used to put cars on huge car transporters. You can also find ramps next to flights of steps for people in wheelchairs to use.

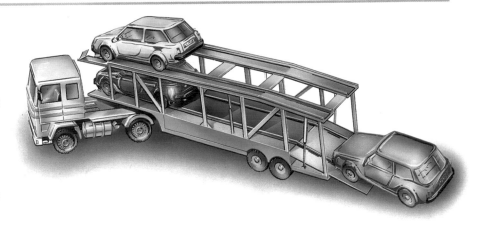

A screw is a kind of ramp

When you turn a screw you twist its thread a long way — by going round and round — to get the screw to go a little way forward. You make the work easier by twisting with a small effort through a long distance.

The screw's thread is like a gently sloping path around a thin cylinder. You can see this idea by rolling a paper 'ramp' shape around a pencil.

How a screw-jack works

Engineers use jacks to raise parts of bridges and buildings, millimetre by millimetre. A motorist uses a jack to raise a car when a wheel has to be changed. You can make a working model of one kind of lifting jack.

Support one end of the brick on the pile of books and the other on the cotton reel, nut and bolt. Using the spanner, turn the nut anti-clockwise. Each time you turn it, the brick is pushed up a little way. Use the spanner to get more leverage on the nut (i.e. to turn it with less effort). You are using a combination of two simple machines, (a ramp and a lever), which is called a compound machine.

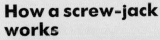

YOU NEED:

- a large, long bolt, with a fitted nut
- a cotton reel
- a spanner to fit the nut
- a housebrick
- a pile of books

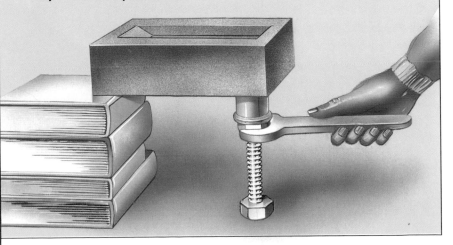

CRANKS

A crank is a special sort of lever. It is used to obtain a large turning force by applying a much smaller effort. In the past a crank was used to wind up a rope on to a drum, to haul a heavy bucket of water from a deep well.

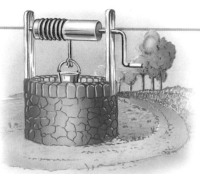

Cranks turned by human muscle power were once used where electric motors are used today. Years ago washing machines were worked by turning a crank!

Experimenting with a crank

Get an adult to help you bend the knitting needle into the zig-zag shape of a crank machine using the pliers.

Ask a friend to grip the crank at the top with the pliers. Put the rubber band around the crank, near to the pliers at the top. Try to turn the crank by pulling on the band. The amount by which the rubber stretches will give you a good idea of how much force you need.

Pull the band down the crank, away from the pliers. Pull on the band again. Judge how much less effort is now needed to turn the crank.

axle

force arm

handle of crank

YOU NEED:

- a long metal knitting needle
- pliers
- a rubber band

What has happened?

It was easier to turn the crank when the rubber band is at a point furthest away from its axle (the part gripped by the pliers). The distance from the axle to where you hitched the rubber band is called the force arm. The longer this is, the less effort you need to turn the crank. But your hand has to push round in a large circle to make the thin axle go around once.

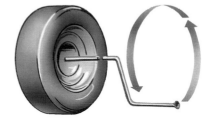

Did you know?
A wheel and axle is a crank in disguise. Or, if you prefer a crank is a simple form of wheel and axle. Why do you think that farm carts and tractors need such big wheels?

YOU NEED:

- a screwdriver with a fat handle

Using a screwdriver

Grip the blade of the screwdriver by the fingers of one hand and hold the shaft with the other.

Try to turn the blade by twisting the shaft (the axle) of the screwdriver. Then try by twisting the handle. This is much easier.

What has happened?
The screwdriver resembles a wheel and axle, or crank. By turning the handle, you were able to apply your effort some distance away from the shaft-axle. The handle gave a longer force arm, so your small effort was more effective.

TRANSMITTING FORCES

Simple machines, such as levers, cranks and pulleys, can transmit forces. They connect the places where you or a motor actually push or pull, to where these forces can do useful work. For example, the handle of a spade upon which you pull is connected to the blade where your force is magnified to push up the soil.

Turtle racing

Cut two turtle shapes out of the cardboard and put a hole in the middle of each. Tie the pieces of string to two table legs and thread a turtle on to each piece. Now race your turtles with a friend from one end of the string to the other. By jerking the string you pass on your forces and make the turtles move along. The strings transmit your forces to the turtles.

When you made the flagpole (pp5) you used cotton reel pulleys with a connecting 'belt' of string to transmit pushes and pulls and make the flag go up and down. Machines are often driven by pulleys connected by belts.

Tests with model drive belts and pulleys

Ask an adult to help you nail the cotton reels and tins on to the wooden bases. There are many ways in which you can position them. Here are some ideas for connecting the 'pulleys' different ways, with the rubber band 'drive belts'.

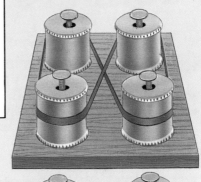
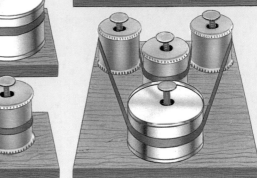
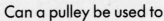
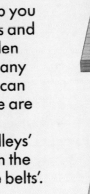

Can a pulley be used to
- change the direction of a turning force?
- to make another pulley go faster or slower?

Gears

An important way to transmit power in a compound machine, such as a car or a kitchen food mixer, is to use gears.

Turn the crank and watch the toothed gear wheels turning. When you work the crank by turning it around from top to bottom, it drives the gears around from side to side.

Mark a spoke of each of the two mixers with the felt-tipped pen. Count how many times each mixer turns when you turn the crank once. Which turn faster, the crank or the mixers? Do both mixers turn the same number of times? Do they both turn in the same direction?

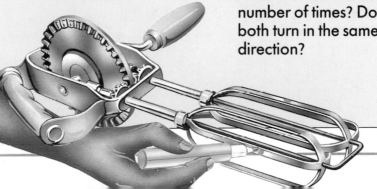

A COMPOUND MACHINE

A tin opener that takes the top off a tin without leaving a jagged edge is a compound machine. It is a combination of a simple wheel and axle machine and a simple lever machine. A bicycle is a more complicated example of a compound machine.

Can you find any other examples of wheel and axle machines?

The chain and sprocket transmit your force from the pedal cranks to the back wheel. When you squeeze the brake handles, forces are transmitted to the brakes, via steel cables. Each pair of brakes that acts on the rims of the wheels is a pair of simple levers.

Turn your bicycle upside down with the saddle and handle bars on the ground. Look for these examples of wheel and axle machines. The main wheels and their axles.
The twin pedal cranks.
The toothed gears, called sprockets, that are connected by a chain drive.

Testing the gears
When you turn a pedal crank in full circle, how many times does the back wheel go around:
- in top gear?
- in middle gear?
- in bottom gear?

Did you know?

In top gear, your force drives a bicycle directly. This is suitable for keeping your bicycle going at a fast speed. In bottom gear, your turning force on the driving wheel is magnified to get you started, or to get you up a hill.

The force of friction

When two surfaces rub together they push against each other with a force called friction. When using a machine, you always have to use up a little energy just to overcome the friction between its moving parts. An important way to lessen friction in a machine is to use a lubricating substance, such as oil.

Oil reduces friction in a machine by keeping the surfaces of its moving parts separated. If you have a bicycle, be sure to keep its moving parts well lubricated.

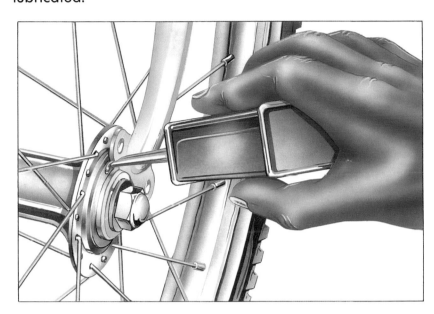

Testing friction

YOU NEED:

- an empty music cassette case
- two rubber bands
- a cork-backed table mat

Rest the cassette case on the smooth surface of the mat. Tilt the mat. Notice how steep the slope has to be before the case starts to slide down. Repeat this test on the rough side of the mat.

Fix the rubber band around the cassette case. Do both tests again.

What has happened?

When the rubber-bound case was tested on the rough surface of the mat it gripped far better than on the smooth surface because of greater friction.

On a bicycle, rubber-lined brakes get a good grip on the wheel rims of the machine, because of friction. Rubber tyres get a good grip on the road and rubber handlebar grips enable you to get a firm hold on them. Friction makes your bicycle safer.

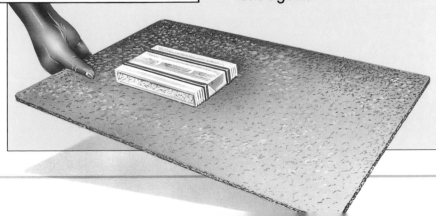

MACHINES AND WORK

To a scientist, 'work' has a special meaning. It means getting a force to move something. Whenever work is done, energy is used up. A machine is used to make work easier. It does so by letting a small effort be used to raise a heavier weight or to exert a greater force.

When you used the spade lever machine (p.4) you made its blade push heavy soil through a short distance, by pulling its handle with a smaller force through a greater distance. About the same amount of work is done by the blade as by you pulling the handle. This is because work, or energy used, is measured by multiplying a force by the distance through which it acts.

Ideally, but never in everyday life, a big force (e.g. weight of soil) × a short distance = a smaller force (e.g. your pull) × a longer distance.

Some energy is always used to cancel out friction.

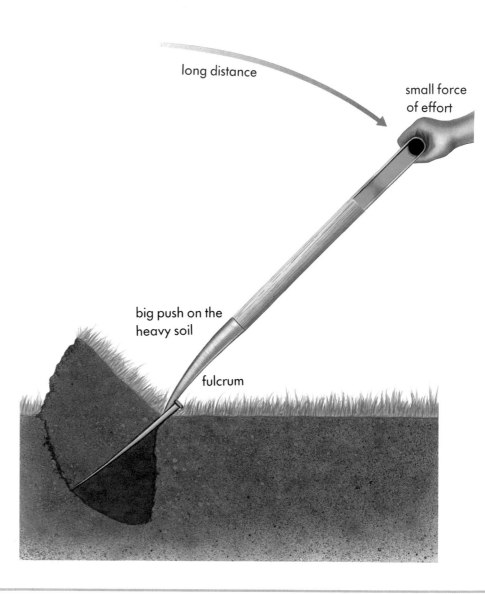

long distance

small force of effort

big push on the heavy soil

fulcrum

How to lift a chair with a broom

Ask an adult for permission and help. Support the stick between the widely-spaced chairs. Get somebody to help you balance the broom against the chair as shown in this picture.

Rock the broom very gently. You will see that the heavy chair moves up and down a little way when you move the broom head up and down a long way. The chair is much heavier than the broom head. How do you think this is connected with using a garden spade?

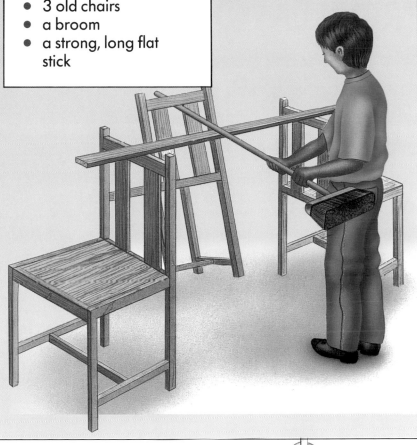

Work done using a pulley system

A newton (N), named after the famous scientist Isaac Newton, is the international unit of force.
work done = force × distance
$40 N \times 1m = 20 N \times 2m$
This is an ideal case. In reality, you would need to pull harder (more than 20 N) to overcome the friction between the rope and pulleys and between the pulleys and their axles. Oiling the axles would lessen your work.

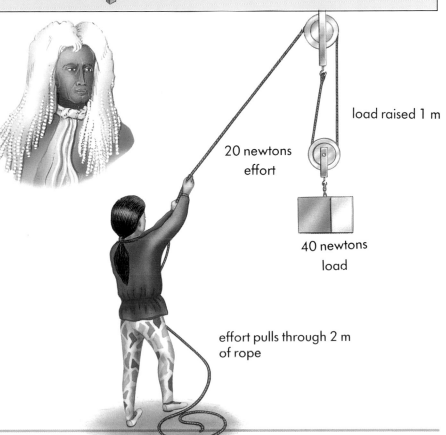

20 newtons effort

load raised 1 m

40 newtons load

effort pulls through 2 m of rope

SOLVING THE PROBLEM OF FRICTION

You have seen how friction is useful for a bicycle (p19), and how, even with a bicycle, it can also be a problem. Oiling the chain and axles helps to solve the problem. But friction in the axles can also be reduced by having steel ball-bearings in the wheel hubs (like the ones you might have seen in the handles of a skipping rope).

Model ball-bearing

Remove the lids from the tins. Fill the groove around the rim of one tin with marbles. Balance the other tin, upside-down, on the marbles, with the edges of its groove resting on the marbles. Balance the book on top. Now spin the heavy book on the marbles. Be careful! You should be able to do this quite easily because there is less friction with rolling than with sliding.

YOU NEED:

- 2 wide tins with press-on lids
- some marbles
- a book

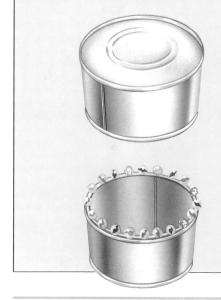

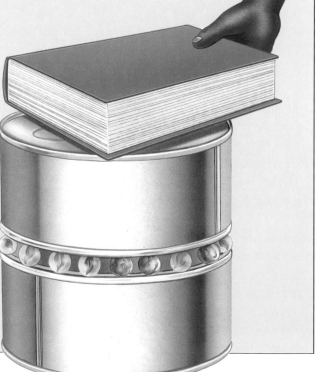

Reducing friction with rollers

Make a hole 6 mm in diameter in one end of the box. Put the balloon in the box with its neck poking out of the hole. Blow up the balloon. Put the box on a table and let the air out of the balloon. Does the box move much?

Repeat the test, but put the box on some pencil 'rollers'. Because the rollers reduce friction between the box and the table, your box should now whizz across the pencils.

YOU NEED:

- a shoe box
- a balloon
- some pencils

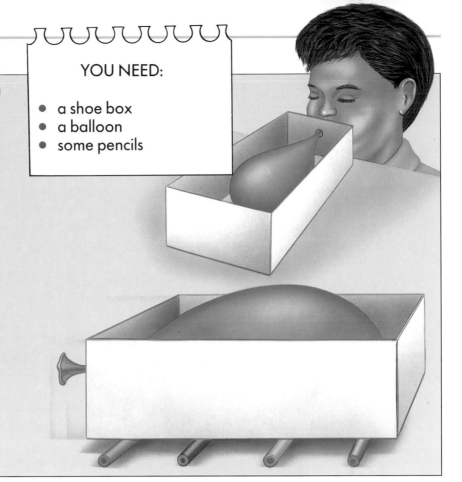

How a hovercraft reduces friction

YOU NEED:

- a large plastic funnel
- a plastic tube or wide straw
- a tray

Push the funnel across the tray with your fingers.

'Listen' to the friction as it scrapes across the surface.

Hold the plastic tube inside the top of the funnel and

blow down gently. The funnel behaves like a hovercraft by rising and sliding quietly sideways.

What has happened?

The pressure of your breath acted on all the inside parts of the funnel and on the part of the tray under the funnel. This provided enough force to lift the funnel, so reducing friction. Air spilling out unevenly from under the 'skirt' of the model hovercraft made it move sideways. A real hovercraft is driven and steered by propellers and rudders.

MORE ABOUT FRICTION

Friction and 'drag'

Tape the end of one of the paper strips to one of the cotton reels. Roll the strip on to the reel and tape the paper down so that it cannot come undone. Tape the end of the other strip to the other cotton reel, but do not roll up the paper.
Go outside in calm weather. Hold the reels together and throw them both away from you.
Which reel goes furthest?
Do the test several times.

What has happened?
The reel with the paper strip wound around it went the greater distance. This was because the reel trailing its paper strip met with more air resistance or drag. Drag is caused by friction with gases and liquids, such as air and water.

Did you know?
The frictional force of drag acts to slow things travelling in air or water. The shapes of cars and the hulls of ships are specially streamlined to lessen the effects of air or water drag when they are moving.

A climbing toy

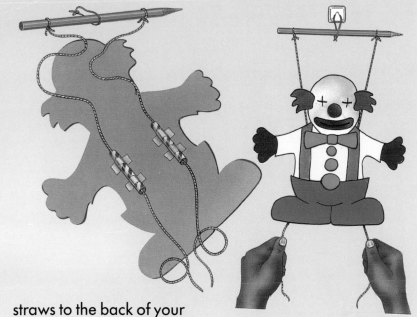

YOU NEED:

- thin string
- a drinking straw
- sticky tape
- scissors
- stiff cardboard
- a pencil and crayons

Cut the cardboard into the rough shape of a clown, bear or monkey. Colour it in. Then tie two long lengths of string to each end of the pencil. Cut the straw in half and thread one half on to each piece of string. Tape the straws to the back of your clown. Tie a loop of string in the middle of the pencil so you can hang it up.

Now make your clown climb by pulling down first on one string, then on the other, and so on. Friction between the string and the straws stops it from slipping back down as it climbs.

YOU NEED:

- uncooked rice
- a jar (which is wider in the middle
- a clean wooden ruler
- a tray

The incredible Indian rice trick

Put the jar on the tray. Fill it to the brim with rice. Pack the rice down with your fingers.
'Stab' the rice with the ruler. You will feel the rice grains packing tighter.

Finally, give the rice a last quick stab and lift the ruler carefully.
With practice you should be able to lift the jar of rice holding the ruler only. Be careful — only lift the jar a few centimetres from the tray.

What has happened?
Friction between the rice grains jammed them together in a firm mass, enabling them to grip the ruler and hold the weight of the filled jar.

WORKING MILLS

Before steam-engines and electric motors were invented, energy to drive machinery in workshops was supplied by wind and water power.

YOU NEED:

- 2 thin straws
- 1 fatter straw
- scissors

Straw mill

Cut the fatter straw in two pieces, about a third of the way down, so that you have a short and a long piece. Cut four slits in the small piece, and bend the strips out to form the sails of a tiny windmill. Twist each sail slightly anti-clockwise. Thread this piece on to one of the thinner straws.

Make a slit near one end of the longer piece of the fat straw and thread it on to the other thin straw. Thread the piece with the sails through the slit. Your mill will spin in the slight breeze. Air drag on its 'tail' will keep it turned to face the wind, like a weather vane.

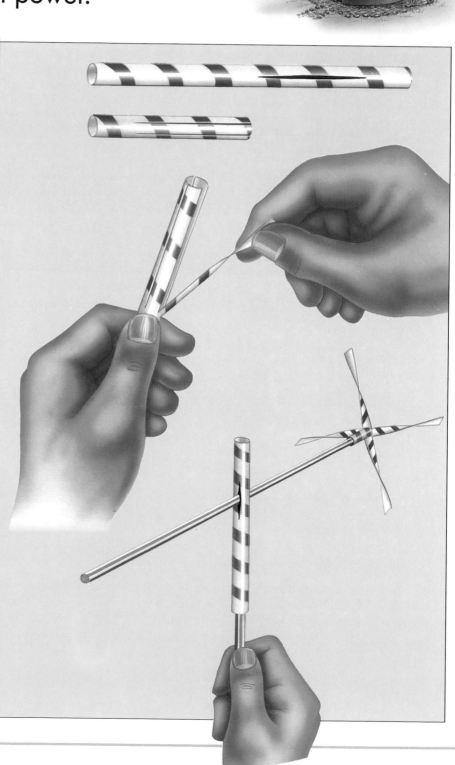

Plastic windmill and watermill

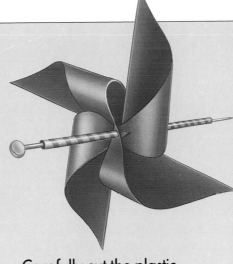

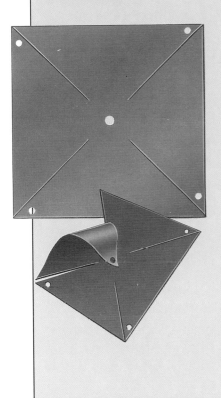

Carefully cut the plastic into a square, about 20 cm by 20 cm. Make a hole in the centre and a hole in each of the corners. Make four diagonal cuts from each corner to the centre of the square, stopping about 3 cm from the centre hole. Poke the straw through the hole in the middle of the square. Thread the corners with holes on to the straw. They need to fit tightly, so do not have the holes too big. Mount the mill loosely on the knitting needle. Blow it, and watch it spin.

Try holding your mill under a tap. It should turn when you trickle water over it. If you turn the tap on too fast, the water will splash, so be careful!

Using the wind to raise a toy

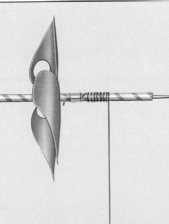

Tie your toy on to one end of the cotton. Tape the other end of the cotton to the straw of the windmill. Grip the pointed end of the knitting needle. Go outside and let the wind drive the mill. As it spins, it acts like a wheel and axle. The force of air pushing on the wheel-like mill produces the turning force on the axle that winds up the cotton and lifts the toy.

With the cotton wound up, hold the mill still. As the toy falls it gives back energy to the mill, making the sails turn slowly.

MORE THINGS TO DO

Drinks can 'roly-poly'

Cut a cardboard circle with a small hole in its middle to fit inside the rim of the drinks can. Shape a short piece of wire into a hook. Ask an adult to make a hole in the bottom of the can using the scissors. Loop the rubber band over the matchstick. Poke the free end of the band through the hole in the can. Tape the stick to the outside.

Use the hook to get hold of the end of the rubber band inside the can and pull it to the opening at the top of the can. Poke the straight part of the hook through the cardboard circle and the bead, and then twist it around the pointed end of the knitting needle. Wind the knitting needle round to twist the rubber band inside. Put your roly-poly on the floor and watch it roll away.

What has happened?

As the rubber band unwound itself and the knitting needle lever pushed against the floor, the force from the rubber band made the roly-poly crawl along.

By putting tight rubber band 'grippers' on the can, can you get your roly-poly to climb over books left in its way?

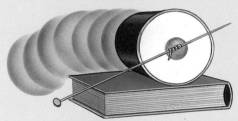

Archimedes screw

Wind the tubing around the rolling pin, to make a spiral. Hold the coils in place, using the sticky tape. Dip the device in a bowl of water and start twisting.

As you watch, you see water being 'screwed' up the tube. You should find it easy to see how a screw is really a ramp wound around itself with this device!

Did you know?

Two thousand years ago, the Greek scientist Archimedes invented a machine based on the idea of the screw. Even today it is sometimes used for raising water. A similar idea is used to transport grains and lumps of solids.

Delaying the big bang with friction

Wind half of the wire around the thick nail to make a stiff spiral. Bend back the other part of the wire to form a right angle with the spiral.

Tie one end of the string to a hook somewhere that is high up (such as on a door). Thread the spiral on the string, with its 'tail' uppermost. Make the string taut by tying its other end to a heavy object on the floor.

Fix the peg on the wire tail. Use the Blutac to fix the pin, with its point downwards, below the outer end of the peg. Blow the balloon up and put it next to the heavy object, under the pin. Slide the spiral up the string. The weight of the peg makes the spiral press against the rough string where it is held

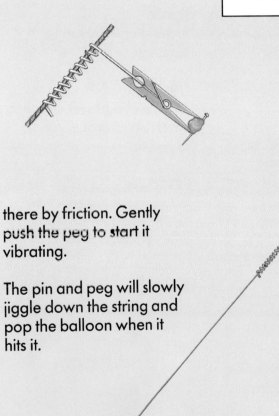

there by friction. Gently push the peg to start it vibrating.

The pin and peg will slowly jiggle down the string and pop the balloon when it hits it.

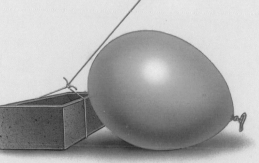

GLOSSARY

B

ball-bearing
A metal ball used to reduce friction in a machine.

C

compound machine
A complicated machine made by combining several simple machines.

crank
A simple form of wheel and axle machine.

D

drive-belt
A loop between pulleys, for transmitting a driving force.

E

effort
The driving force that acts on a machine.

energy
What has to be used if work is to be done.

F

force
A push, pull or twist or squeeze.

friction
An opposing force that acts when two surfaces rub together.

fulcrum
A point around which a simple machine can turn. (Also called a pivot.)

G

gear
A toothed wheel that can engage with one or more others, to pass on rotary motion and force.

gravity
A pull exerted on a mass by any other mass.

H

hovercraft
A vehicle that moves by sliding on a cushion of air.

J

jack
A mechanical device for raising huge weights a little at a time, using a small effort.

L

lever
A rod or bar that can swing around a fulcrum to transmit and magnify a force.

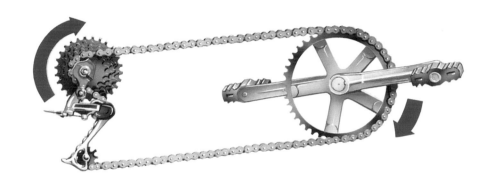

load
The force that is overcome with the aid of a machine.

M

machine
A device for making work easier.

N

newton ('N')
The international unit of force.

neutral gear
When gears in a machine are separated so that they cannot transmit a force.

P

pulley
A wheel around which passes a string, rope or belt.

R

ramp
A slope used as a machine to make work easier. (Also called an 'inclined plane'.)

S

screw
A machine resembling a ramp wrapped around itself.

system
A collection of parts that work together as one.

W

wheel and axle
A machine with which a force is applied to the edge of a wheel is magnified by the axle. A crank is a simplified wheel and axle. A wheel by itself, used as a roller, can also be thought of as a simple machine.

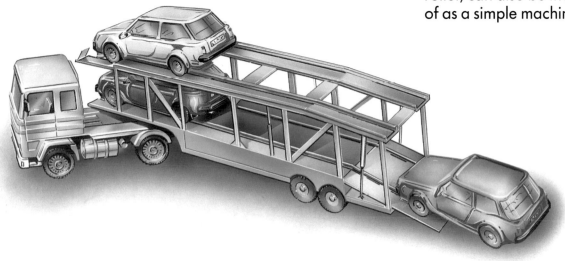

INDEX